A story about dog adoption

Once upon a time there was a little dog.
His name was Chili.

He loved to play in the snow!

Chilli loves being with our family.
We love Chili and we take
good care of him.

But, there was a problem.

When his owners went to school...

...Chili was very lonely.

When his owners came
home from school,
Chili was HAPPY!

One day, our family decided to get
Chili a new friend.

His name is Chex
He came from a
shelter in South Carolina.

But it took a while for
Chili to get used to Chex.

...soon Chili and Chex
were best friends!

Chex was getting used
to living in our home.

He was part of the family.

They love to go on different adventures together!

Both dogs are very, very silly!

I wrote a poem about Chex in school.

Chexeboo

Oh, Chexeboo
How I love you!
Your eyes twinkle
but sometimes you sprinkle
on the floor.
And every time
I open the door
you run out!
So I
let out
a shout
"Come back!"
I go running
and when I get to you
I pet you and say...
"Chexeboo, I do love you!"

Written by Lindsay Jouet

...and Chili was jealous.

But not too much, because he also LOVES Chex.

THE

END

CPSIA information can be obtained at www.ICGtesting.com
Printed in the USA
LVIW01n1949211116
513938LV00006B/64

9 781530 072323